Our **WILD**™ **WORLD**
SERIES

Vultures

Text and Photographs by Wayne Lynch
Illustrations by Sherry Neidigh

NorthWord Press
Minnetonka, Minnesota

IN TIMES GONE BY, many people viewed vultures with respect and admiration. The ancient Egyptians worshipped vultures as gods. Mayan kings in Central America wore jewelry shaped like vultures, and Haida Indians in British Columbia carved vultures on their totem poles.

Worldwide, there are only 22 kinds, or species (SPEE-sees), of vultures. Compare this number with 222 different types of hawks and eagles, 61 kinds of falcons, and 212 kinds of owls. Even though there are not many kinds of vultures, the birds are very successful. There is at least one species of vulture on every continent, except Australia and Antarctica.

If you really love to watch vultures, the best place in the world to live is in Africa where there are 11 species. In the United States there are only 3 kinds of vultures: the turkey vulture, the American black vulture, and the California condor.

On a cool morning, the American black vulture can pull its neck feathers up to cover the back of its head to keep itself warm.

Several hundred turkey vultures and American black vultures may use the same overnight roost.

A Ruppell's griffon vulture lowers its legs as it is about to land near a carcass.

Biologists (bi-OL-uh-jists) are scientists who study animals. They divide vultures into two groups. One group is called Old World vultures. This group includes the 15 species of vultures that live in Africa, Europe, and Asia. The second group, called New World vultures, includes the 7 species that live in North America, Central America, and South America.

The two groups of vultures look alike and behave in the same way. All of them are large birds of prey (PRAY), which means they eat other animals.

One difference between the two groups is that they do not belong to the same scientific family. New World vultures are cousins of long-legged storks. Old World vultures are related to hawks and eagles.

Another difference is the kind of habitat they live in. Old World vultures live mainly in open areas such as grasslands and deserts. There are not many trees hiding the ground, so when the birds are flying overhead they can easily spot dead animals. New World vultures live mostly in tropical rain forests where there are many trees and where the ground is difficult, or impossible, to see.

In those habitats, three New World vultures—turkey vulture, lesser yellow-headed vulture, and greater yellow-headed vulture—have a special talent to help them locate food. They can smell well. This is something very few birds can do.

These vultures can find a dead animal on the forest floor just by following their noses, even when the carcass (KAR-cus) is hidden under grass and leaves!

None of the Old World vultures has a good nose. This explains why there are no vultures living in the tropical rain forests of Asia or Africa. The dense trees would prevent them from finding a meal.

Black-backed jackals and spotted hyenas often compete with vultures for a carcass.

It is easy for most people to recognize a vulture. Most vultures have no feathers on their head or neck, or only fine down feathers that resemble cotton wool. The reasons they look the way they do may surprise you.

Vultures
FUNFACT:

The people in the small town of Hinckley, Ohio, love vultures. Every spring they have a Buzzard Festival to celebrate the annual return of turkey vultures to their area.

Young king vultures are mostly brown. It takes four to five years for the birds to grow the beautiful plumage (PLOO-mij) of an adult.

Even without head feathers the birds are very colorful. A turkey vulture's head, for example, is bright red, and the Egyptian vulture in Africa has a lemon-yellow face and beak.

Other vultures are even more colorful. The white-headed vulture of Africa has a white cap, pink face, powder-blue jaws, and a red beak.

The most colorful vulture is the king vulture of Central America and South America. The skin on its neck is bright orange and yellow, its head is a mixture of purple and red, its eyes are white with a red ring around them, and it has some orange skin hanging from the base of its bill. Many wildlife artists think the colorful king vulture is more fun to paint than any other bird of prey.

The large flap of skin above the beak of the Andean condor is called a comb. It identifies the bird as an adult male. Adult females do not have a comb.

A vulture's bare head helps the bird in several ways. If a vulture becomes overheated because it has been sitting in the hot sun too long it can simply increase the blood going to its face. This gets rid of some body heat and cools the bird.

A vulture can also use the colors in its face to quickly tell other vultures what kind of mood it is in. For example, the facial colors of a hungry, excited vulture are usually much brighter than they are when the bird is calm. The same thing happens when people get angry and their face turns red.

Probably the most important benefit of having a naked head is that it helps the vulture keep clean. When vultures feed on carrion (CARE-ee-un), which are decaying animal bodies, their heads can become dirty and smeared with dried blood and rotting bits of flesh. With bare skin on its head it is easier for a vulture to wash and clean itself after eating than if its head were covered with feathers.

All vultures are big birds, and some of them are very big. Even small vultures, such as the turkey vulture, American black vulture, and hooded vulture, are three times heavier than the common American crow.

The largest vultures could eat two crows in one meal. Some of the biggest vultures are the Andean condor, the Eurasian black vulture, and the bearded vulture. All of these large vultures live high in the mountains in South America, Asia, and Africa. These birds can weigh more than 20 pounds (9 kilograms), which is the weight of a large Thanksgiving turkey.

The smallest vulture in North America is the American black vulture (top) with a wingspan
of 4 feet 6 inches (1.4 meters). The turkey vulture (middle) has a wingspan of about 6 feet (1.8 meters).
The largest vulture is the Andean condor (bottom) whose wingspan can be over 10 feet (3 meters).

Being a big bird has advantages. At a carcass, a big vulture can bully foxes, jackals, and other small animals, and take most of the food for itself. Also, a big bird can last longer between meals than a small bird can. Because dead animals are usually scarce and difficult to find, vultures must often wait many days between meals.

All vultures can go without eating for at least one week and still stay healthy. Some of the largest vultures can even go two weeks or more between meals. When they find food, however, all vultures stuff themselves. Because vultures are such big birds, they can gulp down three or four days' worth of food in a single meal. And they can do it in five minutes!

Lappet-faced vultures often proudly display themselves on a carcass.

The turkey vulture gets its name because its naked red head looks similar to the head of the common barnyard turkey.

Another good thing about vultures is the large size of their wings. The long, wide wings of the Andean condor of South America are the largest wings of any bird. The Andean condor has a distance from wingtip to wingtip, called the wingspan, of 10 feet (3 meters). A wandering albatross has a slightly longer wingspan, 11 feet (3.4 meters), but its wings are narrow and much smaller in total area than those of the condor.

Vultures
FUNFACT:

The largest flying bird that ever lived on earth was a kind of vulture called a teratorn. It lived in South America during the Ice Age. It had a wingspan over 22 feet (6.7 meters), and weighed 175 pounds (79 kilograms)!

No bird of prey uses the power of the wind better than vultures. They are masters at finding winds and using them to soar high into the sky.

One soaring Ruppell's griffon vulture in West Africa flew into a jet airliner at an altitude of 37,000 feet (11,000 meters)! That is about 7 miles (11 kilometers) high. The air temperature at that altitude is a very icy −50 degrees Fahrenheit (−45 degrees Celsius).

Vultures rarely flap their wings when they are flying. Most of them cannot flap for more than one or two minutes without becoming exhausted.

Vultures never waste energy flying like that. Instead, they depend almost completely on soaring when they fly. A vulture soars, or glides, easily. In fact, it is almost as easy for a vulture to soar as it is for it to stand quietly on the ground.

Vultures
FUNFACT:

The legs and feet of many New World vultures are black, pink, or red, but they look white when the birds squirt their liquid droppings on themselves to cool off.

It is not easy for a turkey vulture to take off for flight. Once in the air, its average speed may be 25 miles (40 kilometers) per hour.

The large feathers on the wingtips of the white-backed vulture give the bird forward speed. The rest of the wing area gives it lift.

Vultures are called scavengers (SKAV-en-jers) because they mostly live off dead animals. Sometimes lions, leopards, hyenas, bears, wolves, foxes, ravens, hawks, and eagles may also feed on dead animals. For these animals, scavenging is only a part-time job. For most vultures, however, scavenging is a full-time way of life. They do it better than any other group of birds or animals.

Vultures are good at scavenging for three important reasons. First, when they soar, they get a wide view of the land. Second, when they see a carcass they can get to it fast. Some vultures can glide downward at nearly 100 miles (161 kilometers) per hour. This is much faster than any running scavenger, such as a hyena or a fox.

The third reason vultures are good scavengers is that they hunt in the daytime. Many animals that die of disease, old age, or starvation, die at sunrise. This is usually the coldest time of the day or night and an animal that is very sick may become chilled at this time and die.

Vultures hunt during the day. This means they have the whole day to find the carcass and make a meal of it. The other scavengers hunt mainly at night. While they are snoozing during the day, vultures find many carcasses and pick them clean.

Many people think that vultures survive by cleaning up the scraps from kills made by lions, hyenas, and other meat-eating animals, or carnivores (KAR-nuh-vorz). This is not true. Although vultures often gather around carnivores that are feeding at a kill they actually get very little to eat from those carcasses. Vultures get most of their food from carcasses they find themselves.

Hunting vultures often search in groups. The birds spread out across the sky, each one searching a different area of the ground. When a bird sees a dead animal, it swoops down as fast as it can fly. If no other vulture is watching, it can feed on the carcass by itself, but this rarely happens. Vultures watch each other almost as much as they watch the ground.

Turkey vultures may feed on dead seabirds that the tide
washed ashore the night before.

In East Africa, vultures are found in large numbers.
As many as 60 may arrive at a carcass in just five minutes.

When one vulture sees another vulture drop suddenly from the sky it immediately glides over to see what the cause was. This sends a signal to other birds nearby. Soon, there may be dozens of vultures soaring toward the carcass from miles (kilometers) around. As many as 36 American black vultures have been seen gathering at the carcass of a dead cow. Several hundred Eurasian griffon vultures may be attracted to a dead camel.

The largest groups of vultures are often seen in Africa. Researchers there once counted 250 Cape griffon vultures and over 1,000 white-backed vultures feeding on the bodies of 3 dead elephants that had been killed by poachers.

Vultures
FUNFACT:

Vultures are the only birds of prey that commonly sleep together in large groups. In Florida, as many as 4,000 turkey vultures and American black vultures may sleep in the same clump of trees.

A Ruppell's griffon has found a carcass and two lappet-faced vultures are fighting over which one gets to keep it.

Most vultures that live in the New World, especially the king vulture and the American black vulture, do not have a good sense of smell. Instead, they watch turkey vultures and yellow-headed vultures that do have a good sense of smell. Then they follow them and steal their food. Just three or four American black vultures or a single king vulture can easily bully a turkey vulture.

When vultures first arrive at a carcass they may not eat right away. The animal lying there might still be alive. A bird that is too eager to eat could be injured if it rushes in too soon. The hungriest birds are usually the least patient. Sometimes one or two of them may peck at an animal to see if it fights back. Often they will attack its eyes. If the animal does not move, then the birds that were waiting to see what would happen may suddenly rush onto the carcass.

While eating, most vultures fight with each other, shove, hiss, peck, and scratch. The fights, the noise, and the dust make feeding vultures more exciting to watch than any football or hockey game!

Because many vultures may try to feed at the same time, each bird eats as fast as it can. A lappet-faced vulture can stuff itself in 15 minutes. A Cape griffon can do the same in 5 minutes. The fastest feeder is the African white-backed vulture, which can tear off and gulp down about 3 pounds (more than 1 kilogram) of meat in 2 minutes flat.

Vultures
FUNFACT:

Vultures prefer carrion that is only one or two days old. They often eat rotting flesh that would make other animals sick. They can do this because they naturally have a very strong acid in their stomach that kills many dangerous bacteria.

Warm air helps birds soar. A lappet-faced vulture often must wait two or three hours after sunrise before the air is warm enough for it to soar easily.

The bulging pink crop on the king vulture is a signal to other vultures that the bird is full.

The birds do not actually swallow the food into their stomach right away. They store it in their throat in a stretchy sac, called a crop. When a vulture's crop is full you can see a big bulge at the base of its neck. It looks as if it has swallowed a grapefruit.

Usually, the skin covering the crop has no feathers on it and is often brightly colored. Andean condors have yellow skin covering their crop, king vultures have pink, and turkey vultures have red.

Biologists think that the colorful bulging crop is used as a clue to let other vultures know when a bird is full. A full bird is less likely to fight back when another vulture tries to push it out of the way at a carcass.

An African impala, which is approximately the size of a white-tailed deer, has about 85 pounds (38 kilograms) of meat on it. That is enough meat to feed 40 or 50 vultures. However, 200 of them may gather near a carcass for the meal, so most of them go hungry.

Many of the vultures that get nothing to eat are the ones that arrive late. The others are juvenile vultures that have not yet learned how to fight for their share. Even after there is nothing left to eat but skin and bones, some vultures remain for two or three hours. They may lie in the sun or clean and straighten their feathers. For young birds, carcasses may be an important place to learn and practice vulture behavior.

The heavy, strong claws on a turkey vulture are best designed for walking and grabbing, not killing.

Vultures do not have the strong grip and long, sharp claws called talons on their feet that eagles and hawks use to kill live prey. Even so, some Old World species and some New World species are able to kill prey with their tough feet and sharp beaks. In fact, the white-headed vulture of Africa often hunts and kills live animals this way, rather than search for dead ones. The white-headed vulture takes stranded catfish, and also attacks adult and young flamingos, baby gazelles, young ostriches, bat-eared fox pups, tortoises, hares, and lizards. These bold vultures may even attack a dangerous rock python or a puff adder, a deadly venomous snake.

Biologists have found that vultures eating termites is funny to watch. Sometimes during the African rainy season, dark clouds of flying termites fill the air and thousands more cover the ground. The insects are fat, juicy, and good to eat.

Once, scientists watched 70 lappet-faced vultures, 2 white-headed vultures, and 12 hooded vultures feeding on termites together. That day, these noble birds of prey did not look fierce or scary. The big birds behaved more like barnyard chickens chasing the tiny insects on the grass and picking them up one by one with their beaks!

When a hooded vulture is near a carcass, its flushed red face indicates that the bird is excited.

Turkey vultures may sun themselves together on a ledge. They can also watch for food below.

Although vultures are sometimes thought of as being dirty, this is not really true. All of them spend two to three hours each day nibbling and preening their feathers.

Every day many of them gather along sandy rivers, around desert waterholes, or next to mountain pools to wash. In Central America, researchers watched a dozen king vultures bathe together in a pool above a waterfall.

In Africa, as many as 100 white-backed vultures may gather and rest beside a river. Hours earlier, these same birds may have fed together at a carcass where they scratched and pecked each other wildly. At the river, they are quiet, peaceful, and friendly.

After bathing, they often stretch out their wings to warm and dry themselves. The birds may use the same washing areas day after day, sometimes for years.

Lappet-faced vultures display to each other during courtship. It helps the female see which mate would be the best.

Vultures take a long time to mature. Turkey vultures and American black vultures do not find a partner until they are at least 3 years old. Egyptian vultures wait until they are 4 or 5. Condors, griffons, and lappet-faced vultures stay single until they are 6 or 7 years old. Once a vulture chooses a mate, however, the two usually stay together for life. Vultures may live 15 years or more.

Vulture courtship is not very exciting. Male vultures do not sing beautiful songs to their mate. They only hiss, snore, and grunt. They never bring the female gifts of food. They do not nibble on their mate's feathers in a gentle way. Male vultures don't even show off with fancy flying tricks. Some of the New World vultures may puff up their colorful necks and dance around a little, but vultures are generally quite dull when they are courting.

New World vultures and Old World vultures choose different places for their nests. All of the vultures in the Old World build nests of sticks, and they line the inside with dry grasses. Usually they build their nest in the top of a tree or on the ledge of a high cliff. Most of the nests are easy to see.

Some of the tree nests may be very large. The lappet-faced vultures probably build the largest ones. Their nests can be up to 6 feet (2 meters) across and 3 feet (1 meter) deep. They are strong enough for a person to stand in them.

In East Africa a white-headed vulture (left) and a white-backed vulture (right) may share a lookout perch.

New World vultures prefer their nests to be dark and hidden. Most of them are difficult to find. In fact, no researcher has ever found the nest of a greater yellow-headed vulture. Only about six king vulture nests have been found.

New World vultures commonly hide their nests in caves, in hollow trees, under tangles of vines or brush, or among piles of rocks. Turkey vultures in Canada often nest in the attic or upper floor of an old, abandoned farmhouse. The birds come and go through broken windows.

New World vultures do not build nests. They lay their eggs directly on the ground. Most vultures are shy when they are nesting and usually choose locations far from people who might disturb them.

Vultures
FUNFACT:

Vulture parents feed their chicks mouth-to-mouth. As soon as
the hungry chick pecks at the parent's beak, the adult bird vomits
up a hot meal from its bulging crop. The young bird
takes the food directly from the back of the parent's mouth,
or sometimes even reaches deep into its parent's throat.

African white-backed vutures gather dried grass to line the inside of their large nest.

The turkey vulture builds no nest. It lays its beautiful speckled eggs directly on the ground.

Vultures are like most large birds that live a long time. They lay very few eggs. All large vultures lay just one large white egg often marked with brown or rust spots, streaks, or speckles. If you made an omelet with the super-size egg of a lappet-faced vulture it would be the same size as one made with six chicken eggs. The three small vultures—turkey vulture, Egyptian vulture, and American black vulture—lay two eggs each. Their eggs are only one-third the size of a big vulture's eggs.

Hawks, eagles, falcons, and owls care for their young in a certain way. Once the female lays eggs, she gently sits on the nest and covers the eggs to keep them warm. This is called incubating (INK-you-bait-ing). The male hunts for the two of them.

When those chicks finally hatch, the female continues to stay in the nest. For several weeks after the eggs hatch, she huddles over the small, downy young to protect them and keep them warm. This behavior is called brooding. During this time, the father hunts for the whole family.

Only after the chicks are about half grown does the mother start hunting again to help the father feed their hungry, growing family.

Vulture parents, however, both take turns incubating, brooding, and feeding the chicks. While one parent warms the egg or chick, the other one hunts for meals. Every one or two days, they switch jobs.

Vultures
FUNFACT:

Some of the cliff-nesting vultures in the Old World, such as the Cape griffons and Ruppell's griffons, form large nesting colonies. In East Africa, one colony of Ruppell's vultures has 4,000 birds in it.

At about one month old, turkey vulture chicks are down-covered.
Feathers are just starting to grow on the wings.

The eggs of many falcons, owls, and hawks usually take about 30 days to hatch. Vulture eggs take longer. The eggs of the smaller vultures hatch in about 40 days, and those of the larger ones hatch in 55 days.

Vulture chicks never seem to leave home. Whereas young hawks and owls leave the family nest in about 4 to 6 weeks, many vulture chicks stay in the nest for 16 to 20 weeks. Even after they leave the family nest, many vulture chicks are fed by their parents for another 16 weeks. Some adult vultures feed their chick for almost one year!

One of the main reasons that vulture parents care for their chicks so long is that scavenging is a difficult thing to learn. Even with their parents' help, only 2 out of 10 young vultures live to be one year of age. Most die of starvation. Others fly into power lines or are killed on highways when they try to feed on road-killed animals. A few accidentally eat poison, and some are shot.

Biologists place colored tags on the wings of California condors
to identify the birds and to help them watch where the birds fly.

Twenty years ago, many vultures were in serious trouble. Today their future is a little brighter. For example, the California condor almost disappeared from the skies of the American West, and at one time there were only 22 birds left. Today there are over 200 condors. Nearly 100 of them are once again flying free in the skies of California, Arizona, and Baja, Mexico. The remainder are living and breeding in zoos.

In recent years, both American black vultures and turkey vultures in eastern Canada and the northeastern United States have moved north and expanded the area in which they live, called their range or territory. The birds are now more common than ever.

There is more good news from Europe and Africa where biologists and landowners have set up vulture "restaurants" to feed the local birds and help them survive. Vulture watching has even become a tourist attraction. Many people in southern Africa visit these vulture feeding stations to get a close look at these magnificent birds of prey.

All of this news is good, but there is also some bad news. In India, more than 95 percent of all the Indian white-backed vultures and long-billed griffons have died in the past 10 years. The reason for this was a big mystery that was solved only recently.

At first, researchers thought the cause of the birds' deaths was some kind of disease, insecticide, or poison. The reason turned out to be an unusual poison.

The vultures started dying after eating dead farm animals, something they had done in India for hundreds of years. The difference now was that many of the dead animals had been given an anti-fever drug just before they died. When the vultures ate the carcasses they were slowly poisoned by the drug.

The disappearing vultures in India have caused some unexpected and serious problems in that country. With no vultures cleaning up the dead animals in the countryside, the number of wild dogs has increased greatly, because there is more food for them to eat.

Wild dogs often carry a deadly disease called rabies. Dog bites from rabid dogs can kill people. Today in India, about 30,000 people die from rabies every year, and this number is expected to increase.

Indian white-backed vultures used to be very common. Today they are very rare.

This example shows how humans are still connected to the other living things in the natural world. When one small part of this world is damaged or destroyed, humans may suffer because of it.

We must remember this lesson and use it to protect vultures and the other wild creatures in the natural world. If we do this, we may also protect ourselves.

Many turkey vultures spend the winter in Florida.

Internet Sites

You can find out more interesting information about vultures and lots of other wildlife by visiting these Internet sites.

www.adoptabird.org/	Adopt-A-Bird
www.EnchantedLearning.com	Disney Online
www.ggro.org/idhelp.html	Golden Gate Raptor Observatory
www.pbs.org/wnet/nture/exbirds/warriors.html	PBS Online
www.raptor.cvm.umn.edu/	The Raptor Center at the University of Minnesota
http://endangered.fws.gov/kids/index.html	U.S. Fish and Wildlife Service
www.animal.discovery.com	Discovery Channel Online
www.audubon.org	Audubon Society
www.kidsgowild.com	Wildlife Conservaton Society
www.nwf.org/kids	National Wildlife Federation
www.tnc.org	The Nature Conservancy
www.worldwildlife.org	World Wildlife Fund